A New Beginning
The Rededication of
Mosque Maryam

The Honorable Minister
Louis Farrakhan

ISBN: 979-8-9859218-6-1

EDITOR'S NOTE

The Honorable Minister Louis Farrakhan delivered this message on October 19, 2008, as the culmination of a special interfaith program wherein he rededicated Mosque Maryam in Chicago, Illinois.

The edited transcript of this lecture is marked with subheadings to facilitate the careful study of the words of the Honorable Minister Louis Farrakhan.

CONTENTS

INTRODUCTION

Sheikh Ahmed Tijani delivered the adhan (Islamic call to prayer) from the balcony of Mosque Maryam. Behind him sat the ceremonial orchestra let by conductor Charles Veal, Jr. The English translation of the adhan was delivered by the narrator for the program and could be heard through loudspeakers on the mosque property. The program featured a special rendition of Ave Maria by Grammy award-winning vocalist Stephanie Mills. Prayers in their faith tradition were then offered by a Hebrew Israelite priest, Christian pastor, and Muslim Imam.

The following text was displayed in a slideshow during the introductory part of the rededication program.

This Mosque is named after Mary, the Mother of Jesus. She is given great distinction and honor in the Holy Qur'an because she gives birth to the Messiah, who carries the indwelling spirit of Allah (God), manifesting Allah's (God's) Presence, which allows Jesus, the Messiah to do that which no prophet or messenger did before him.

He gives sight to the blind by Allah's (God's) Permission. He makes the deaf to hear by Allah's (God's) Permission. He gives life to the dead by Allah's (God's) Permission. It is written in the Holy Qur'an concerning Mary, that she was purified by Allah (God) and chosen by Him above all the women of the world. She is more honored in the Holy Qur'an than the mothers of Abraham, Moses, and Muhammad. None of these mothers of the prophets, no matter how great their sons were, was given the distinction of having a chapter in the Holy Qur'an named after them.

In the history of Islam, when the early Muslims were being persecuted in Arabia due to their new faith, some of them migrated to Abyssinia (Ethiopia), a Christian country in Africa. The persecutors of the Muslims followed them to Abyssinia (Ethiopia) to encourage the Negus (King) to expel the Muslims and send them back to Arabia to sure persecution and death. The Muslims were brought before the Ruler to be questioned and they recited out of the chapter in the Holy Qur'an called "Maryam" (Mary).

When the Ruler heard their recitation of this part of the Qur'an and of their belief in Jesus, son of Mary, as the Messiah, the Negus (King) said, "We believe the same," and he allowed them to remain in his country.

The Honorable Minister Louis Farrakhan has named this Mosque after the Mother of Jesus to let this dominant Christian country know and understand that every Muslim believes in Jesus.

In The Name of Allah, The Beneficent, The Merciful. We give Him praise and thanks for His Goodness and His Mercy to the human family, that whenever any member of the family strays from His straight path and loses His Divine Favor, before He punishes, He always raises from among that people a prophet or a messenger. He gives that prophet that which is called divine revelation. By means of that divine revelation, He calls the people back to the path of righteousness that He might once again bestow on them the blessing of His Favor.

We thank Allah (God) for all His prophets, all His messengers, all His saviours and wise men who have come to the people of our planet. Most of all, we thank Him for Musa or Moses, and the Torah. We thank Him for Jesus and the Gospel. We thank Him for Muhammad and the Qur'an. Peace be upon these worthy servants of Allah (God).

I am a student of the Most Honorable Elijah Muhammad. I could never thank Allah (God) enough for intervening in our affairs to bring us back to His straight path, in the Person of Master Fard Muhammad Who came among us and raised from among us one to lead, teach, and guide us as His messenger to us, the Honorable Elijah Muhammad.

I greet all of you, my dear Brothers and Sisters, with the greeting words of peace. We say it in the Arabic language, *As Salaam Alaikum*. My dear Brothers and Sisters, this has been a very emotional moment for me to hear music in the mosque for the first time in 20 years. I thank Allah (God) so much.

Immutable principles of truth

That sound that we heard from the shofar, the ram horn, which announces Rosh Hashanah,

Yom Kippur, and Shabbat or the Sabbath, calling the people of Israel to purification and preparation for atonement for sin and wrongdoing, that we may keep Allah's (God's) favor to us. We thank those who come by the sound of the bell to Christian worship, and the Black man from Ethiopia named Bilal who created from the Spirit of God that which is called the *adhan* or the call to prayer. These three branches of pure monotheistic belief that spring from a father, Ibrahim or Abraham, who was a man who fought against polytheism.

There is a story in the Qur'an about the idol worshippers of his day. There were three of them, one of them larger than the others. It is written that Abraham in the night knocked down one of the idols. The next morning, the people asked, "Who did this?" Then Abraham said, "Ask the big one. He should be able to tell you." They were upset with Abraham, and they boiled him in oil.

So, we must be careful how we take down the idols that people worship. But it is misplaced

3

worship that has the human family at odds with each other. While the prophet was among us, there was unity among the Jews. When Moses was among them, unity. When the prophet was gone, division came. The Holy Qur'an says [Surah 42:14] that they did not become divided until after knowledge came to them, splitting up their religion into sects and parties, vying with one another due to envy.

This happened during the time of Jesus. It happened again during the time of Muhammad, peace be upon him (PBUH). It happens every time there is a charismatic person who guides people sometimes to a new truth. When that person dies, then that terrible human condition arises when people seek power. Greedy for power and out of envy, they war with one another over who will sit where or who will go there. Then, the People of God become divided.

Allah (God) says in the Qur'an, He sent messengers and prophets to every nation. He didn't send messengers and prophets to every nation to preach a different religion. Otherwise, we could charge Him with being the author of confusion, while the scripture says God is not the God of confusion but the God of peace. How did we become so confused?

When a messenger or prophet of God came in different parts of the world, they always brought a truth to correct the problems of that time. Those contemporary truths were founded on immutable principles that never change. So, the prophets all over the earth taught the same basic truth.

When the prophet died, people began to name the message after the prophet. We have Confucianism, Taoism, Shintoism, Zoroastrianism. Some would call Islam Muhammadanism. Christianity, Judaism. But what is the real message or religion of Him Who created the heavens and the earth, and gave every creature the true religion? What is that? When you see the creatures, each creature follows a path that is indicative of the nature of that creature. All of God's creatures He gives to each a way. What is the way that He gave to the human being?

Did He change? Did He wait until 2,000 years ago to give man the way? Did He wait until 1,400 years ago to give man the way? No. From the time He created men, He gave him the right way. Allah (God) says in the Qur'an [Surah 30:30]: "set your face for religion, being upright, the nature made by Allah in which He has created men."

The Way of our Creator

Look at our planet. Look at how we have become so divided, so hateful, yet claiming the same Creator. Do you think that Almighty God is happy with Christians and Muslims and Jews claiming Abraham, the Upright One, yet destroying each other every day because we think we have the right way? Is that really the right way?

Allah (God) created Adam. All the scriptures of Torah, Injil, and Qur'an talk about Adam. Did God give him the way? You call it religion. He doesn't even mention such a thing. That's man's invention. What is your religion? What is *your* religion? *What* is your religion? No. What is the nature in which God created you—that is The Way. That is the right way, but most men know not.

When God created Adam, He gave him the right way. What was that? He said, Adam, eat from all the fruit of the trees in this garden, but this one in the middle of the garden, this tree you should not eat. It seems like when God or our parents tell us what we shouldn't do, suddenly we get a drive. "I wonder why Mama told me not to do that? I wonder why God told us not to do that? I think that's the very thing I want to do."

There is something in human nature that makes us desire to do what pleases us against the wise counsel and guidance of God. The real religion of God is this: Obey My commands. That's the right way. What do you want of me? Guide me.

We just got here, some of us, and some of us are ready to leave. We are so wonderful in the way we treat our automobiles. I just bought a new Lexus or Ford or Cadillac or Mercedes-Benz or BMW. In the glove compartment, there's a little manual.

If you want to sustain the life of this car, you change the oil at this time; you grease it at this time; you do this at this time. Some of us are very dutiful. We love our cars.

Do we think that we know better of how to live a life that we did not give to ourselves? Shouldn't we think that He Who gave us life is the best qualified one to instruct us on how to live the life that He gave? How did we become so wise after just being here a few days?

There is One Who has no birth record, Who is older than the sun, moon, and stars, Who knows the nature of you and me, and knows what will protect us and what will destroy us. But the thing that God has done out of His love for and respect for the human being, God says in the Bible [Genesis 1:26-27]: I created man after My likeness and in My image. That's big. Very, very big.

If God created you and me after *His* likeness, no wonder when the disciples of Jesus said to him, Master, when were you hungry and I fed you not; when were you naked and I clothed you not; when were you out of doors and I gave you no shelter; when were you sick and imprisoned and I ministered not unto you, that Jesus said: "Inasmuch as you have not done these things to the least of these my brethren, you have not done it also unto me" [Matthew 25:42-45].

We love to make over big shots. "Do you know who I met yesterday? Do you know who was in the restaurant when we went to have dinner? I saw so-and-so big shot." When you left your house, you left a big shot when you left your mom and your dad. When you walked the street and you saw a homeless person on the corner asking for help, you may not have known it but he's a big shot too. He doesn't know it. When you walk by the prostitute who doesn't really know who she is or how valuable she is, you walk by a big shot that is in need of service. But we have been trained to look out for those who don't really need us and walk by the people most in need.

Prophet Muhammad (PBUH) one day was talking to a well-placed man. He was engrossed in conversation with this man. A blind man was tapping his way up to the Prophet. The Prophet looked on him because he disturbed the conversation and the Prophet frowned. But the Qur'an says [Surah 80:1-10] Allah (God) frowned and said to the Prophet, you are talking to a man who really is wasting your time, but the man who is most in need of your service, you turn away.

Transforming human life

May I humbly say, religion as it is being preached and practiced is a failure. Not some of them, all of them. Don't be displeased with me. We must judge failure and success by how effective we are in transforming human life, not how happy the people are over our preaching or the song that we sung, or the prayer that we said, and then they go back out in the world to be the same as they were before they came to that house of worship.

When Jesus came on the scene, there were many preaching the law. But Jesus said, "O ye hypocrites." That's a tough word. Who wants to be called such an ugly name? He said you have whited sepulchers and in them are the bones of dead men. The churches, mosques, and synagogues are white, meaning they look pure on the outside but the people on the inside are like the bones of dead men and dead women. What does that mean? Every religion has rituals. Every religion has a way of devotion that may be peculiar to that faith tradition.

In the prayer that Abraham and Ishmael made when they reconstructed laid the foundation of al-Kaaba, the holy house at Mecca, they asked Allah (God), "Show us *our* way of devotion." There was a way of devotion peculiar to them.

In every part of the world, the way of devotion that God gave people is sometimes

11

concretized in rituals. The ritual itself is not the truth. The ritual is the embodiment of the truth, but when you become ritualistic—I wonder if you understand. I'm sure you do.

In Islam, we have been commanded by Allah (God) to perform five daily prayers. We were taught through the example of Prophet Muhammad (PBUH), the way to pray. From the outward appearance if we all follow the way of the Prophet, it looks like we are following him. But there's a difference between "looks like" and "what really is" in worship.

I can raise my hands and say, "Allah-u-Akbar, Allah-u-Akbar!"—God is great. But If God is really great in my life, my life will reflect obedience to what He has commanded. If I say ritualistically God is great but I am too—"You told me to do this, but I really want do that"—then God is only great in the words we say but not necessarily in the life we live.

In our prayer service, which is so beautiful, we bow. At a certain point in the prayer, we make *sajdah* or we prostrate; we redo the fetal position. In that position, we are at our lowest and our words of God are, "Glory to Allah, The Most High." When we submit totally to God, we are always humble. This is a very powerful word, "humble." Humility before honor, humble to God. When you bow down to God, you give Him a chance to exalt you.

The Bible asks [Matthew 6:27], can anyone add one cubit to their height? When you have on stilettos, they make you feel taller. At night, after a hard day in stilettos, you are so glad to get those things off your feet to come back to reality. I cannot add anything to who and what I am; neither can you. Titles don't add to you. Titles can sometimes take away from you by making us think we are what the title says. We run for titles, but we don't run for qualification. I'm sneaking up on something.

Rituals of religion. Prayer is ritualistic. We should perform it. The Qur'an says Allah (God) loves those who are mindful of their prayers when they pray [Surah 23:1-2]. Sometimes you pray and it's just a formality. The Qur'an says that when Allah (God) makes something tough for us, we make our prayer sincere. You can pray but you don't pray like when you are in deep trouble.

When we get in deep trouble, that's when our prayer is really sincere. Look at the words that come out of our mouths: "Lord, if You get me through this this one time, I promise You I will serve You for the rest of my days." Even in those words, it is indelibly put in your nature to serve your Creator.

What will happen when we don't need rituals anymore? When the truth of a ritual is made known, the ritual loses significance. We, as Muslims, must once in our lifetime make a pilgrimage to the holy city of Mecca. Some of us have been very blessed to make that journey. When we make that journey, we all should know that everything that we do is a sign of something bigger.

When we walk around al-Kaaba seven times, when we kiss the black stone, when we run between the hills—signs of something bigger. When we are in the Plain of Arafat and it is hot, hot, hot, we stay there for most of the day in heat and prayer and thoughts about the oneness of God. Then we journey to Muzdalifah, and we stone *shaytan*. I was there. I picked up stones and, boy, was I throwing them. I shouted *Allah-u-Akbar* so loud, people stopped throwing and looked at me.

Throwing stones at a stone that represents *shaytan* or the devil or Satan is not the same as actually hurling truth at falsehood or fighting against the demons within ourselves. When Muslims say *jihad, jihad, jihad*, it's a great sounding word but it terrifies others. "You mean you're going to kill us who are not Mooslems?" No, it doesn't mean that at all. *Jihad* only signifies the greatest of all struggles—the struggle of the human being against the wickedness of self.

Oneness with God

Now I will say what this new beginning is for the Nation of Islam. I know you're concerned and you're curious. I will give you a picture and then I will explain. In the Qur'an [Surah 22:5], it says God created you from a small life-germ and then you became a clot, and then you became an embryo, and then you became a fetus, and then you were brought forth from your mother's womb, complete yet incomplete.

Along that journey we, as human beings, are evolving, going through stage after stage on our journey to become complete human beings. When you mature to be a grown-up man or woman, are you yet complete or do you yet have a distance to go to complete your real journey, which is the journey of life itself? What is that journey? The Qur'an keeps telling us about "those who deny the meeting with God." Our journey is from a tiny life germ to become one with our Creator.

This is why the man Jesus in the Bible is so great a human because in his journey, though he lived a short time, he accomplished something that some of us can live 100 years and never accomplish.

He accomplished oneness with God. When the disciples and Jesus were together, they asked [John 14:8-9], "When will we see the Father?" He said, "Have I been among you all this long and you have not seen Him. When you see me, you see the Father; for I am in the Father and the Father is in me. Me and my Father are one."

It is the same with Prophet Muhammad (PBUH). According to the history, he was the most obedient to the Will of God. That's how you attain oneness with God. God cannot give you the secret of nature unless you please Him to that degree that He can open the secret of nature for us.

There are many preachers, teachers, sheikhs, mullahs, and scholars who read our Bible and Qur'an and we say, "The Lord spoke to me last night." When we are asked, "What did He say?" it doesn't mean He didn't. It means that if He communicated with you, the world has the right to know what He said. Don't say what Moses said, tell us what He said to you last night. If He didn't say

17

something new, if He didn't reveal to you something that was not known before, then maybe you need to stop saying what you can't prove.

The musicians played Bach, and they will play something of Beethoven. When you play something written by someone else, you may know the notes and play the notes, but you can't get out of it what is in it because you're not in tune with him who wrote it. When you want to play the composition of one who wrote something, we need to ask what was his state of mind when he wrote this? What were the circumstances of his life when this came from him?

With God, many of us read His books and hear His words and we call ourselves interpreters. But no one can interpret the Word of God properly if our hearts are not in tune with Him and His Will.

A universal change

Something has happened in America. We have churches. We have mosques. We have synagogues. But the streets are filled with crime, violence, the abuse of women and children right outside the church and right outside the mosque. If our religion is only for the walls and the people within them, then we have failed.

We have spent money to make a beautiful building but that is not what God is interested in. If we don't make beautiful people to come in and out of that building doing the Will and the Work of God, then all of this means nothing.

To those who are here from different religions and different races, I'd like to say something to you about Black people, if you don't mind. Our people are in a very, very bad condition. I don't care how many cars we drive or homes we have or money we have, the condition of our people is really an indictment against the leadership.

If we really are in tune with the prophets and they're writings, religion should never lose its power to transform. In the Book of Isaiah, he says, "there will be a new heaven and a new earth, and the former things will pass away." In the Book of Revelation, a man is talking—a man—he says, "Behold, I make all things new." I'm coming to the new beginning. That's a heck of a statement: Behold! "I"—personal pronoun. Make—not some things—*all* things new. Then he says, there'll be a new heaven and a new earth, and the former things will pass away. We're lined up then to see big change. Big, big, big change.

If you notice, change is the theme in the race of the presidency. That theme, regardless of who says it, is resonating with the people because deep down in the hearts of the people they are totally and thoroughly dissatisfied with government, and they are seeking real change. But the change that will feed our hearts is not necessarily a political change. The change that will feed our souls is that which is coming on the scene today—it is a *universal* change.

Where do we fit? If He's going to make all things new, does that mean Judaism will be made new? Christianity will be made new? Islam will be made new? We will be made new? What does it mean "all things"—that's everything. God is dissatisfied with everything. Will there be new government? New constitution? Will there be new people in power? Will that be you? Will that be me? Will that be him? Will that be her? We don't know, but we know this: Change is absolutely necessary.

Yes, there will be a new heaven and a new earth. The Honorable Elijah Muhammad said that's both spiritual and physical, real. The sun is dying. The moon is dying. The planets have a life span. We won't be here. You don't need to worry about the change in the heavens, neither your children or your children's children, or your children's children's children's children's children's children. That will take place, but we won't be here.

The Honorable Elijah Muhammad said that the change that it's talking about is a change in the spiritual rulership and a change in the political rulership. Paul said [Ephesians 6:12-13], "We war not against flesh and blood but against principalities and powers and the rulers of the darkness of this world and spiritual wickedness in **high places**.

What ruler wants to be changed? People in power want to hold on to power and they will lie, they will steal, and they will kill to hold on to power. That is why most political leaders walk on red carpets—red for the blood that was shed to put them in power and red for the blood that is shed to keep them in power.

When I used to visit Libya, my Brother Gaddafi was a revolutionary. They wanted me to join the Mathaba or the part of the government that deals with revolution. Of course, Farrakhan had a different thought. I told them no.

Revolution made at the point of a gun is not revolution; that's just a change in leadership probably from one thief to another. They may start off good, but the kind of power you take from the gun, you will continue to use the gun. Then dissatisfaction will continue to grow in the people, and they will remove that government.

Separation of church and state

America has a marvelous system. They say they stole an election a few days ago, but this is a great system. However, something is wrong, terribly wrong. The founding fathers of this democracy were men who believed in God. They didn't treat us so nice, but they did believe in God. The constitution that they wrote, they really wanted government to be run not so much by religion, neither did they want the type of separation of church and state that America is suffering from right now.

What kind of state is this that these religious people who are here today, they are invited to the City Council to say the prayer and then get out. That sounds awful, but it is true. You can say the prayer at the Senate, "We're opening with prayer. Say the prayer and get out."

I praise Jewish schools because they have to remember God in their schools and have to pray in their schools. In the Catholic tradition, it is the same. In the Muslim tradition, it is the same. But the public

23

schools are suffering because God has no place in them. All kind of wickedness is seen in the public school system.

What are you teaching? "I teach biology." Who created that that you study? Who created the amoeba? Who created any life form that you are studying to call yourself a biologist? Is it not He Whom you don't want to have His Name mentioned? He's the real headmaster.

You're studying physics, chemistry, and history but the God Who is the Author of it all, you can't mention His Name. Then, something is wrong in a system like that.

For the record, the founding fathers wanted separation of church and state, but not disconnection of the church from the state or the state from the church. Do you realize that all throughout the Bible and Qur'an, God respected kings, but He sent prophets to kings. The prophets always said to the king, "Thus sayeth the Lord." Today, however, the prophets are bought by the kings. Therefore, if you're looking for a favor from the kings, you don't want to talk too much so you muffle your mouth so you can get a favor from the ruler. But then you're not seeking the favor of God, you're seeking the favor of man, so you lose the favor of God. What happens if there's a disconnect between heaven and earth?

If the sun does not draw water up from the earth's surface into the Earth's rotation, which is called gravitation, forming what is called a cloud; and if the wind does not drive that cloud over an earth that is dead and rain down on that earth so that the seeds in the earth may swell and germinate and come up that we may eat and feed from the earth because there's a connection between what is above and what is beneath.

We don't have that connection anymore. That's why the human being is suffering and is a caricature of what God intended human beings to be. We are no longer "man in the image of God." We are a caricature of what God intended because we are all filled with rebellion. Whatever Allah (God) said thou shalt not do, government says it's OK. Help yourself. The confusion is so great.

The condition of Black people

You, my Brothers and Sisters, when Elijah Muhammad came among us, he taught what you could call a "Black Theology." A lot of people were offended and turned off by that. In the Muslim world, they were angry and said Islam does not teach color, what's wrong with you people. They don't know what happened to us.

One of the members of the Virginia House of Delegates [Henry Berry on January 20, 1832] said, "We have extinguished every avenue by which light can enter the slaves' mind. If they continued along that line, Black people would be in a condition that we could never come out of." Look at Black people now, and I am going to ask you a question.

My Arab Brothers and Sisters who are here, you give honor to Prophet Muhammad (PBUH) because he took Arabs from a state of what they call *Jahiliyyah* or extreme ignorance. With this book Qur'an, he raised the Arabs and made the Arabs a power in the world through divine revelation. The Caucasians once lived in the hills and cave sites of Europe. They didn't know how to cook their food or bury their dead. Moses taught them and they came forth from a cave state.

You can say, "By the light of the silvery moon," while White folks say, "I'm going there." You can say, "I wonder is there something going on on Mars." They put together the mathematics and science and have a contraption on Mars. They don't believe in a mystery God. They believe in the reality of God and how God works through the human by giving us insight into the nature of His creation.

Here's a people who have been in America more than 450 years. Foreigners come to America and within a few days they have money. They have businesses. They have economic standing. They're proud of being an American because they came here with nothing, and they have what they have. We've been here longer than anyone else except the native Indigenous people, Indians. We have some stars among us. We do. We have great minds among us. We do. We have people who are shaking the world. We do. But the Honorable Elijah Muhammad said no one man can ever escape being identified with the condition of his people. If your people are nothing, how can you be something? If you don't change nothing into something, then you are just something that is made.

Look at the condition of Black people. *CNN* had a television program about Black people that started off with deadbeat fathers and women who were pregnant from a man but there's no man to help them to support them. That's the way it started. After several days, it ended on the AIDS pandemic, which is in our community more than any other community. According to the program, the Black woman today is the greatest carrier of the AIDS virus.

They went to education. They not only showed how Whites in America are being dumbed down but the most intelligent in America in science and mathematics are people from Asia—India, Korea, China, and Japan. Where are White people? They are down on the list. Where are Hispanics? Further down on the list. Where are Black people? Way further down on the list. This is our condition.

In the Caribbean, the businessmen are Chinese, Arab, and White. They own the businesses. Black folks may be in office, but they are not the owners of the wealth. This is in the Caribbean. This is in Africa. Black people want to do something for self but there is something missing. If something is missing, my question to you is, don't we need somebody to address us and our concerns, to raise us, reform us, transform us, and make us again what God created us to be?

A prophet sent to each people

The Man who came to us from Mecca, we

call Him "Master Fard Muhammad." He had a Black father and a White mother. That Man came to us first because our condition was worse. He was so skillful. He developed a methodology along with an ideology that would start a process of transformation in our lives. I want you to please listen to me. There never were a people considered in scriptural terms as mentally dead. The Arabs were ignorant, but they weren't dead. They were in their own land, speaking their own language. They weren't dead; they were ignorant.

Every people who had a prophet, they were in their land. God raised a messenger from among them who spoke their language and dealt with their problems. The messenger doesn't have to be universal if he is called to deal with a specific sickness in a specific people. Our people are sick unto death, and we need somebody.

Master Fard Muhammad, with a White mother and a Black father, He was able to come in and out of America for 20 years before He even made Himself known to the Honorable Elijah Muhammad. He was among White people. He was in the colleges. He was here, He was there.

He was studying your mind—the mind of the slave and the mind of the slave master—because He had to deal with both minds and both cultures. This may shock some of you, but He wanted to help eventually both people. That message that you call "black supremacy" fed a broken heart, a broken mind, and a broken spirit. As a Caucasian person, sometimes you look at us and may not understand what we've been through that puts us in our condition, so you don't know how to deal with us. **You don't know how to deal with us.** The teachers who teach us in school throw up their hands.

Some of us can function in White society very well. We're acculturated. We're educated. We're stimulated by the wealth of America, and we want it for ourselves. So, whatever we have to do, we adapt. But the masses, they can't adapt. They don't know what this is.

No jobs. The greed of the corporate giants moves factories out of the inner cities into the suburbs and then into foreign countries to get cheap labor. This knocks out the White labor and Black labor. Today the move of enticing our Brothers and Sisters from Mexico and Central America to come here is because they have nothing there. So, this [working in America] is an enticement. Corporate America says, "Our bottom line is thinning out. We must increase our bottom line. Let's get cheap labor from Mexico, Central America, and South America." Our Brothers and Sisters from Mexico are not trying to take your job. They're just trying to survive by coming here. America already knew that they were undocumented, and they didn't care. "We want a bottom line."

Our Mexican Brother and Sister work very hard. Some of our Brothers and Sisters from Mexico and Latin America worked on this building. We didn't have to find them. They were there. They worked hard. But some of us—we work a few minutes, then we talk a few hours, and at the end of the week, we want the money. There's something messed up about that picture, but it is real.

We cannot escape the reality of our condition and want other people to see us as an equal when we cannot qualify for equality. In scripture [1 Corinthians 1:27-28], God said He would choose a foolish people to be His people; He would choose the things that are naught, to bring to naught the things which are. He said [Deuteronomy 28:13], "Thou shall no more be the tail, thou shalt be the head." Then the scripture says [Psalm 118:22-23, Matthew 21:42, Mark 12:11], "This is the Lord's doing and it is marvelous in our sight."

Broken covenants with God

Prophet Muhammad (PBUH) said he heard the footsteps of Bilal, an Ethiopian Black man, going into paradise ahead of his own. How could a follower of a great one precede him into paradise? It doesn't mean that Bilal is going to enter heaven before the Prophet. Whenever you say you are chosen, please don't use such language unless you're going to do what you are chosen to do. Whenever God raises a people from ignominy to greatness, it is because He wants to use that people for a broader, bigger purpose.

The Arabs were chosen by Allah (God) to be the recipient of a prophet considered the greatest, though we don't make distinctions among the prophets. Whoever is greater or lesser, that's by Allah's (God's) command. He gives greater wisdom to some prophets than others but that's not to make one feel better than others. Allah (God) sometimes gives greater knowledge to a prophet for the mission that that man must accomplish. If you have a simple task, you get simple knowledge; if you have a big task, you get big wisdom.

Brothers and Sisters, the Arabs were given this Qur'an and they were told to spread it to the ends of the earth. For the most part, they did their job. The Arabs kept the book, Qur'an, pure. That's wonderful. You get great credit for that, but we failed because we arrogated to ourselves that which made us think that this was an Arab religion. Some of my Brothers, when they hear I'm a Muslim, they say, "We're very happy that you accepted our religion." Stop. I did not accept your religion.

I have re-accepted the nature in which we are created. We didn't need you. We are born Muslims. We thank you for helping us to be ourselves, but don't make us into you. This is what's wrong with Christianity. You want to make people into yourself and deny who they are. You can't make me into you. You *can* encourage me to be the best that I can be.

The covenant is broken with the Arabs. Somebody else will have to lead you now back to paradise. The Prophet himself described him. He said Bilal—that means an African. The Prophet said Bilal would lead him into paradise—he's really talking about the Arabs. You will go but it will be somebody different from yourself that will lead you

35

there. It may be a little difficult for you to swallow. But I'm going to go all around the room.

My Christian family, there's a parable in the Bible that talks about your neglect of these pitiful people who were brought to America to be made slaves. Christian neglect. The parable in the Bible is the Good Samaritan. Don't be offended. I share this out of love.

A man went down from Jerusalem to Jericho. On the way, he fell among thieves who robbed him of his raiment, hit him in the head and left him wounded in the road.

A priest walked by on the other side. He saw the man wounded. He didn't help him. Along came a Levite who came to where he was, looked at him, but did not help him out of that condition.

Along came the Good Samaritan who saw the man wounded, poured oil in his wound, bound up his wound, took him to an innkeeper, gave the innkeeper some money, and said, "If it is more than what I've given you, on my return I'll pay you."

It all started over controversy because Jesus said, "Love your neighbor." One smart fellow asked Jesus, "Who is my neighbor?" Jesus didn't answer directly, he gave them a parable. Please don't be offended. The church walked on the other side. You all really know how to help us. I'm not talking about money. I'm talking about the transfer of knowledge. There would not have to be a Black church if Black people who wanted to go to church were treated well in the church. We would not have had to leave the church. You were First Baptist; we were Second Baptist. We must talk like this to one another, not with hatred or vitriol.

You failed—not us; you failed God. When God gives you wisdom and power, He gives you an assignment that goes along with that. If you walk by the man who needs your help and you know how to help and you won't give it to that man, then how will God feel about you?

The Levite saw him and looked at him. The Levitical priesthood could help raise Black people from that condition because you were once in it yourself. If we are left in that condition to be exploited, then the wrath of God will come down on the church, the synagogue, and the mosque.

Some of our Brothers own stores and they are forbidden to eat the swine, but they will feed it to us. Some of our Brothers are forbidden to take alcohol but they have liquor in their store, and they feed it to us. Some of our Brothers know that Allah (God) taught the Prophet to teach us the respect and protection of our women, but some see the terrible condition of our women and take advantage of them. This is not good.

What is happening to our country now? Have you noticed the weather? Have you noticed the storms? Have you noticed the fire, the floods, the hail, the wind? You don't have power to stop that. America is suffering. The stock market is falling. Your 401(k) is gone. And you wonder what's happening. God is troubling America because America can do better.

All of us, as human beings, can be better than what we are. We can reflect God, or we can be devils. Your color doesn't matter. You can be a devil black. You can be a devil white. You can be a priest devil, a sheikh devil, a cardinal devil, an imam devil, a minister devil. We all have the capacity to do right or wrong.

Cardinal tenet in every faith tradition

This meeting today in this mosque is to celebrate the oneness of God, the oneness of humanity, the oneness of the prophetic community, and the oneness of religion. I had our research team look at all the religions and bring back to me the kernel teaching of every faith tradition. An African traditional proverb is: "One going to take a pointed stick to pinch a baby bird should first try it on himself to see how it hurts." If you took a pointed stick and did that to yourself, would you do it to the bird?

In the Baha'i faith, the kernel of the teachings of Bahaullah is: "Blessed is he who preferred his brother before himself." In Buddhism, the kernel of Buddhist teachings is: "Hurt not others in ways that you yourself would find hurtful." In Confucianism, it is the word *shu*, which means reciprocity: "Do not impose on others what you yourself do not desire." In Hinduism: "Do not to others which if done to thee would cause thee pain. This is the sum or the total of duty." In Jainism: "In happiness and suffering and joy and grief, we should regard all creatures as we regard ourselves."

In Shintoism: "Be charitable to all beings, for love is the representative of God." In Sikhism, the kernel is: "Don't create enmity with anyone as God is within everyone." In Taoism: "Regard your neighbor's gain as your gain and your neighbor's loss as your loss." How many of us are happy when we get something and sad when somebody else gets something? That's sickness. In Zoroastrianism: "Whatever you do not approve for yourself do not approve for anyone else. When you have acted in this manner, you are righteous."

I saved the three Abrahamic traditions for last. In Judaism: "What is hateful to you do not do to your fellow man. That is the entire law. All the rest is commentary." In Christianity: "Do you unto others as you would have them so do unto you." And in Islam: "No one of you is a believer until he desires for his brother that which he desires for himself."

The new beginning of the Nation of Islam is that we evolve beyond just the service to our people. I was with the Honorable Elijah Muhammad one day and he said to me, "Brother, they call me a Black nationalist." He never said he wasn't. He just said that's what they call me. He said, "Brother, Black is not national. Black is universal."

All the time that man was among us he was feeding us, teaching us, and guiding us. I'm sure his family members can bear witness that there were Whites who came to his table, there were Asians who came to his table, there were great imams and scholars who came to his table. He never mistreated anyone. He gave them respect.

At his last sermon to us in 1974, he had two White Muslims on the rostrum with him. One of them was Brother Ali Baghdadi and the other one was a Muslim from Turkey. He said, "These men are not here to see if you are clothed in a long white dress or a long black dress. They are here to see if you are clothed in the principles of your religion."

The unifying Promise of God

The Honorable Elijah Muhammad said Allah (God) did not raise us, Black people in this hemisphere, to be mockers of anyone. He's raising us to be servants of the human family. After the dross has been taken from us, our job and mission is to help bring in a government of peace wherein we all can live together in peace.

Before we can accomplish that mission, we must grow out of the mind of black inferiority and Whites must grow out of the mind of white superiority. Prophet Muhammad (PBUH) said, "There is no superiority of the White over the Black or the Black over the White. The one who is best among you is he or she who is most careful of his or her duty to Allah (God)."

Muhammad and Jesus are the two greatest of those who proselytize the teachings. Jesus and his disciples have spread Christianity all over the world. Muhammad and his disciples have done the same.

Are Muhammad and Jesus enemies? No. Why then are we? Is Muhammad and Jesus an enemy of Moses and the Israelite prophets? No. Then why are we? We all need to rise from this house and all houses like it to teach a message that will inspire, motivate, and stimulate human beings to act so that God may be reflected in us.

Elijah Muhammad said the best religion—he didn't say Islam—he said the best religion, brother, is do unto others as you would have others do unto you and love for your brother what you love for yourself. All the rest of the teaching is based on that principle. When you go forth out of this place today, let us go forth determined to be better tomorrow than we are today. As you drive down the street, don't drive in a way that offends your neighbor. You know how you fight over parking spaces sometimes? Is it necessary? Give it up. "You can have it, Brother. I'll find another one."

What would it take from us to be kind? What would it rob us of to be a better human being? If we start where we are and spread it from where we are, perhaps in our lifetime we will begin, as we are beginning, to see change.

We see change going on in America. We see change going on in the hearts of young Caucasians. They are now instructing their parents. Older people who have the old way, be careful. Moses had some old folks that didn't want to change.

God had given them a land and in that land were some giants. God instructed Moses and Aaron to take them into the land. The people said, "Not us. We're not going up in there. You and your God, go get those giants out of that land, and then we'll go in." Guess what God said? "Fine. I will let you wander in the wilderness until you die out and I will take your children and they will inhabit the promised land."

It is the young people today that every branch of faith should be going after because the Promise of God is not necessarily in the elders. The Promise of God will be found in the young. Thank you for listening. May Allah (God) bless you as I greet you in peace. Now, the prayer of dedication.

Prayer of Dedication

The Honorable Minister Louis Farrakhan:

Bismillaahir Rahmaanir Raheem
[In the Name of Allah, The Beneficent, The Merciful]

Alhamdu lillaahi Rabbil 'aalameen
[All praise is due to Allah, the Lord of the Worlds]

Ar-Rahmaanir-Raheem
[The Beneficent, The Merciful]

Maaliki Yawmid-Deen
[Master of the Day of Judgement]

Iyyaaka na'budu wa Iyyaaka nasta'een
[Thee alone do we worship and Thee alone do we
beseech for help]

Ihdinas-Siraatal-Mustaqeem
[Guide us along the straight path]

Siraatal-lazeena an'amta 'alaihim
[The path of those upon whom Thou hast bestowed
favors]

ghayril-maghdoobi 'alaihim
[not the path of those upon whom Thy wrath is
brought down]

wa lad-daaalleen
[nor of those who go astray]

Oh Allah, we praise You. We thank You. We

honor You and we glorify Your Name for granting us

a chance to be ourselves again. Oh Allah, we thank

You, the Eternal, Omnipotent God, for allowing One

to come to us to help us on the journey back to our

nature. We thank You for the Honorable Elijah

Muhammad who taught us that the words that

Master Fard Muhammad taught, "Be yourself and

accept your own," we have agreed to accept our nature and to be ourselves.

Oh Allah, we thank You for the promise that You made, that we would no longer be the tail, but we would be the head by Your command. Make us worthy to not only be Your servants, but to take the wisdom that You give us and serve fallen humanity.

As Abraham and Ishmael stood at the Kaaba after their work of restoration and asked Allah to make them Muslims, make them submissive to His Will, and raise from among them a nation submissive to His Will, we stand before you today asking the same. Make us submissive to Your Will and raise a nation obedient to Your statutes, laws, and commandments.

As Your servant, the prophet David wanted to build a tabernacle for You, it was in his heart, but You gave that job to his son Solomon. You blessed the house that they built to glorify Your Name. We know that there is no house that can hold You. But we beg You to let Your Spirit be in this house, be among us. Anoint us with Your Spirit and cover our head with the oil of divine knowledge, wisdom, and understanding. In the Temple of Solomon, there was only oil enough for one day to light the eternal flame, but You made that oil to last for seven days.

Seven represents infinity. We ask, Allah, not that You light a lamp with oil, but You light our hearts with the oil of Your Spirit. And let that be a permanent flame, that when we leave Your house, we go out into the darkness of the world, that Your people who walk in darkness may see a great light.

Oh Allah, if we sin or fall short of what You have commanded us and we repent of our wrongdoing, as You have said in Your scriptures, "If my people who are called by my Name will humble themselves and pray and seek my face and turn from their wicked ways, then will I hear from heaven, forgive their sins, and heal their land."

Minister Ishmael Muhammad:

Our Lord, punish us not if we forget or make

a mistake. Our Lord, do not lay on us a burden which Thou didst lay on those before us. Our Lord, impose not on us afflictions which we do not have the strength to bear. And pardon us, and grant us protection, and have mercy on us.

The Honorable Minister Louis Farrakhan:

Oh Allah, we thank You for this day. We thank You for the labor that went into this house. We ask of You, that all those who hear Your Word from this house and houses like it, let it touch their hearts that we may be made new creatures in You. Oh Allah, we beg of You that You protect us in our going out and our coming in. Should enemies come against us, be Thou our protector and our defender, and defend all those who seek to do Your Will. We ask it all in Your Holy and Righteous Name.

We know that this house cannot hold You. We are the real house of God. We desire to let You into us, through our ears and the Word of Yours that is spoken to us. Come into us. Dwell in us that we may become the true Body of the God, the true Body of the Messiah, Mahdi, the Christ. We ask it all in Your Holy and Righteous Name. Amen.

Minister Farrakhan's closing words after the prayer
(the beginning was not recorded on microphone)

… You will find that among people of all faith traditions, there is a model community rising. The unity of all those communities will become the Kingdom of God on earth.

Thank you for your presence. Thank you, all these wonderful pastors, imams, rabbis, people of all races, thank you for honoring us today with your presence. May Allah's (God's) peace and blessings be with all of you, as I greet you in peace.

As-Salaam-Alaikum.

APPENDIX

The History of Mosque Maryam

The following is a transcription of remarks delivered by Minister Ishmael Muhammad during the rededication of Mosque Maryam before his introduction of Minister Louis Farrakhan.

As-Salaam Alaikum. Peace be unto you. Mosque Maryam was originally a Greek Orthodox church built in the 1950's. It was ranked one of the 10 finest churches and houses of worship in the country. The architectural design of Mosque Maryam is a replica on a smaller scale of the Hagia Sophia in Istanbul, Turkey, which was formerly called the Hagia Sophia Church.

The Hagia Sophia Mosque in Turkey was built in the sixth century by the Byzantine emperor Justinian. It holds great prominence and significance to both Christians and Muslims. This house, when it was built, was named St. Helen by the Greek Orthodox Christians in honor of the mother of the

Emperor Constantine I. It was Constantine who united both the eastern and western churches and established the first ecumenical council of the Christian church, and most significantly resulted in the first uniform Christian doctrine called the Nicene Creed. From the Council of Nice, modern Christianity was born and was spread throughout the world.

When this house was first being built, we are told that the Honorable Elijah Muhammad visited the property and stepped foot on the first foundational stones and said to his son who accompanied him, that one day this place would be his. After years of negotiations, the Honorable Elijah Muhammad would finally realize his vision and desire by purchasing it in 1972. After the departure of the Honorable Elijah Muhammad and the succession of leadership to his son Imam Warithudeen Muhammad, the Honorable Minister Louis Farrakhan, in the rebuilding of the Nation of Islam, repurchased the mosque in 1988.

Minister Louis Farrakhan signed the contract at that time without having the actual money in his pocket. With resounding faith, he inspired the Nation of Islam to raise the necessary funds. And within a four-month period, that obligation was satisfied. After the repurchasing of the mosque, additional monies were raised to repair and renovate the mosque.

Artisans from Turkey were brought in to do the exquisite calligraphy work that you see in the dome. Around the ring of the dome are found the verses in Arabic from the 24th Chapter of the Holy Qur'an, entitled "The Light." In the four corners, the Arabic inscription done in 24 karat gold and laid over cobalt blue reads, translated in English, "There is no God but Allah." In the very center of the dome are found the words in Arabic, "Allah is the Greatest."

In 1988, the mosque was dedicated and named "Mosque Maryam" in honor of the woman who is regarded above all the women in the world, Mary, Mother of Jesus.

Twenty years later, we are here this afternoon on the 19th of October, after a year of extensive renovations and work to witness and participate in the rededication of Mosque Maryam.

The renovation involved the replacement of the old roof with a new one, new boilers and air conditioning units were put in, new carpet, restoration of the terrazzo floors and the marble here in the main sanctuary, restoration of the brass, new solid wood doors, painting, plastering, a new front entrance gate, cladding of the steps as you entered into Mosque Maryam this morning with black granite, fountains, water features, a new digital sign, cleaning and tuckpointing of all the limestone, and the placing of a gold dome, which is the only gold dome between here and the sacred mosque in Jerusalem, Al-Aqsa or the Dome of the Rock. This renovation also included our school which is adjacent to the mosque, Muhammad University of Islam. With new school desks for our children, new flooring, ceiling tiles, lighting, and much, much more. On the lower level of Mosque Maryam, you can find our prayer room which in Arabic is called the *musalla*.

We are still awaiting, on ships from China, granite plant urns and granite black chalices. We hope on your return, next time you will see the complete finish, restoration, and renovation of Mosque Maryam.

Materials came from all over the world. The craftsmen and workers that worked on this building came from all races. We thank all the believing members of the Nation of Islam for their skilled labor and all those who worked on this magnificent house. This exquisite and magnificent renovation we hope will be pleasing and acceptable to Almighty God Allah in its service to humanity.

ABOUT THE FINAL CALL FOUNDATION

Final Call Foundation

The Final Call Foundation was established in 2021 with the purpose to support raising awareness, preserving, researching, and amplifying the public works and personal history of the Honorable Minister Louis Farrakhan in the uplift of all humanity.

Follow us: @finalcallfoundation
@FCFcharity

Visit The Final Call Foundation Amazon Author Pages:
www.amazon.com/author/finalcallfoundationhmlf
www.amazon.com/author/finalcallfoundation

Upcoming Title

7 More Speeches by the Honorable Minister Louis Farrakhan

On the Sacredness of The Female

Available Titles

Sarah: Five Notes on a Woman's Prayer over Her Pregnancy
A Study of the Biblical Matriarch of the Children of Israel and Mother Sumayyah Farrakhan of the Nation of Islam

A Demonstration of Love
A special collection of articles and editorials by Dora Muhammad providing a glimpse into the heart, mission, and life work of the Honorable Minister Louis Farrakhan

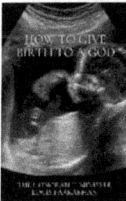

How To Give Birth To A God
A five-part lecture series by the Honorable Minister Louis Farrakhan

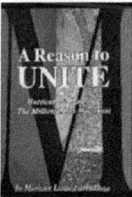

A Reason to Unite
Hurricane Katrina and the Millions More Movement
A collection of excerpts from speeches delivered by the Honorable Minister Louis Farrakhan during a 23-city tour

A Saviour is Born for the Black Man and Woman of America
The first Saviours' Day message delivered by the Honorable Minister Louis Farrakhan in his effort to rebuild the Nation of Islam

ABOUT THE EDITOR

Dora Muhammad is an artist, author, and advocate. She served as editor-in-chief of *The Final Call* Newspaper from 2003-2006. In 2010, she founded The AWARE Project, a multimedia vehicle for advocacy on issues relative to women's awareness, engagement, rights, empowerment, and advancement. She earned a Bachelor of Arts in Journalism and Documentary Photography, with a concentration in Magazine Production and completed her photography thesis at Dartington School of the Arts in Devon, England. She worked as an arts administrator for Autograph-ABP (Association of Black Photographers) while studying International Law and Human Rights at the University of London. Dora earned her Master of Public Administration and has extensive work in government relations and public policy formation. A daughter of Indo-Caribbean immigrant parents, Dora is a native New Yorker who resides in Northern Virginia. She currently serves as the executive director of The Final Call Foundation.

Visit the Dora Muhammad and AWARE Project Amazon Author Pages for a catalog of her books.

www.ingramcontent.com/pod-product-compliance
Lightning Source LLC
Chambersburg PA
CBHW060353050426
42449CB00011B/2961